SHORTIES

Harry Thompson &
Marcus Berkmann

Illustrated by
Eddie McLachlan

CORGI BOOKS

SHORTIES

A CORGI BOOK   0 552 13049 4

First publication in Great Britain

PRINTING HISTORY

Corgi edition published 1986

Acknowledgements to:
Michele Kimber, Gary Pritchard,
Gordon Thompson and Jean Berkmann-Barwis
This book is set in 10/11pt Century Schoolbook

Corgi Books are published by Transworld Publishers Ltd.,
61-63 Uxbridge Road, Ealing, London W5 5SA, in Australia by
Transworld Publishers (Aust.) Pty. Ltd., 15-23 Helles Avenue,
Moorebank, NSW 2170, and in New Zealand by Transworld
Publishers (N.Z.) Ltd., Cnr. Moselle and Waipareira Avenues,
Henderson, Auckland.

Printed and bound in Great Britain by
Cox & Wyman Ltd, Reading

SHORTIES, or, THE SHORT BOOK

by a famous short person.

Hullo. And welcome to THE SHORT BOOK, a celebration of all things diminutive, and their significance in today's fast-moving, high-technology world.

For many years now, men and women of abbreviated stature have been discreetly but determinedly making a profound impact on the fabric of our society – innovating, creating, making the world a better place for all of us to live in. Attila the Hun, Queen Victoria, Paul Daniels – the list is endless.

But despite the achievements of these pint-sized pioneers, it remains incumbent on abridged people everywhere to continue this great work. Our brief as vanguards of the economy-sized movement is to consolidate past progress into a pocket programme for today's community – in short, a knee-high manifesto for the modern world.

Let's be brief – the potential advantages of being short are now more numerous than ever:

* If you get locked out, you can use the cat-flap.
* Half fare on buses.
* Children's clothes.
* Not so far to fall if someone big pushes you over.

In years to come, this concise volume could well

3

become the bible of the undersized classes, giving short shrift to those who seek to short-change us at every opportunity, and promoting the compact cause into a new era of heightened awareness.

Remember – pound for pound, YOU are more likely to succeed than your oversized counterparts. Inch for inch, YOUR achievements will light up the fundament in a way that the lanky majority can never match.

So think short. It's a small world.

© A famous short person 1986

WAYS TO ADDRESS SHORT PEOPLE

RIGHT:

SUCCINCT
COMPRESSED
COMPACT
CURTAILED
REGRETTABLY RESTRICTED

WRONG:

MICROBE
TITCH
MIDGET
TIDDLER
SHORTIE

SOME FAMOUS SHORT PEOPLE

RONNIE CORBETT
MICKEY ROONEY
EMPEROR HIROHITO (The 'Sawn-off Shogun')
PAUL DANIELS
R2D2

WELL KNOWN MISCONCEPTIONS ABOUT SHORT PEOPLE

Chirpy
Sweet
Lovable
Chirpy
Fun to be with
Chirpy

WELL KNOWN FACTS ABOUT SHORT PEOPLE

Aggressive
Self-pitying
Defensive
Violent
Miserable
Short

THE PINT-SIZED CONQUEST OF THE WORLD

A SHORTER HISTORY ATLAS

Short people are never happier than when conquering the world, subjugating huge areas of territory and putting thousands of people to the sword. Here are some notable short world dictators from the pages of history.

* ALEXANDER THE GREAT
* HITLER
* NAPOLEON
* ATTILA THE HUN
* LESTER PIGGOTT

Although control of the entire world has temporarily slipped from the hands of the Undersized, short people are still to be found in many highly significant areas of the globe:

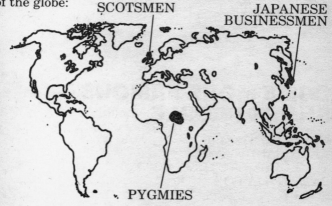

SCOTSMEN

JAPANESE BUSINESSMEN

PYGMIES

TOPICS NOT TO BRING UP IN THE PRESENCE OF SHORT PEOPLE

Most short people find it difficult to relate to their own lack of size. While this is relatively amusing for the rest of us, it is incumbent upon every right-thinking man or woman to treat them with tact and diplomacy. The following is a list of topics to be avoided when one is patronizing a short person.

Basketball results.
The Post Office Tower.
General de Gaulle.
The tall ships race.
Cranes.
Snowdon. (The mountain in Wales. It's perfectly acceptable to mention the photographer).
Hop-picking.
Joel Garner (Somerset & W. Indies).
The Watusi tribe.
Gerry the Giraffe.
Anything on high shelves.

SOME MORE FAMOUS SHORT PEOPLE

NAPOLEON (again)
ALAN LADD
TOULOUSE LAUTREC
SAMANTHA FOX
SOOTY

JOBS SUITABLE FOR SHORT PEOPLE

PIANO STOOL
DOOR STOP
TABLE LEG
GLOVE PUPPET
WORLD DICTATOR
JOCKEY
TV MAGICIAN
PAGE THREE GIRL

SOME THINGS THAT SHORT PEOPLE FIND IT DIFFICULT TO DO

There are still some areas of life that the diminutive have yet to master. Help them out if you can.

CHANGING LIGHTBULBS
SEEING ANYTHING AT FOOTBALL MATCHES
NOT DROWNING IN JACUZZIS
RUNNING AWAY FROM ESCAPED LIONS
THE HIGH JUMP

USEFUL PRESENTS TO GIVE SHORT PEOPLE AT CHRISTMAS

A LADDER

WAYS TO APPEAR LESS SHORT

A GUIDE FOR THE DIMINUTIVE

Avoid double 20 on a dartboard

Wear a sarong

Visit countries full of short people

Jump everywhere

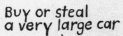

Buy or steal a very large car

BIG 1

Conquer the world

Get a long pet

Buy a miniature
St. Bernard

(TO SCALE)

Stay on at
school

Join a limbo dancing club

13

FUN AND GAMES WITH SHORT PEOPLE!

Contrary to certain shortist propaganda, today's happy-go-lucky short person is always ready with hours of entertainment for his family, friends and colleagues. THE SHORT BOOK is now able to present an exclusive selection of leisure activities utilizing your short person to the full.

SHORT MAN'S BLUFF
An enjoyable game for players over 18.

Blindfold a short person and, on the count of ten, let him into the room: he then has to feel his way around, calling out the names of any objects in his path. Meanwhile, everybody else goes down the pub.

SHORT MAN'S KNOCK
An immensely satisfying game for players of all ages.

Everybody sits in a circle while the short person stands outside and knocks loudly on the door. Nobody lets him in.

SHORTIE IN THE MIDDLE
An immensely dull game for two players.

For this game you will need a field or open space, a large ball (a football or a volleyball will do) and a short person. The short person is placed between the players, who proceed to throw the ball to each other in turn, while the short person attempts unsuccessfully to intercept it.

PLACES TO PUT SHORT PEOPLE

(A GUIDE FOR THE TALLER PERSON)

IN THE LUGGAGE RACK
ON THE MANTELPIECE
IN THE SOCKDRAWER
UNDER THE BED
OUT OF SIGHT

LET'S EAT SHORT!

Having short people round to dinner often poses a serious social problem for the caring hostess. Are there enough cushions? Should you saw six inches off the table legs? Will they be able to reach the doorbell? Now, at last, THE SHORT BOOK offers you the kind of advice you were too embarrassed to ask about.

WHAT TO FEED SHORT PEOPLE
Shortbread
Shortcake
Shortcrust pastry
Petits Fours
Small Fry
Not a lot really

HOW TO GET RID OF SHORT PEOPLE
Announce in a loud voice: 'I hope you short people are going to go home'

HOW TO GET RID OF SHORT PEOPLE WHO OVERSTAY THEIR WELCOME
Call the police.

HOW TO TELL THE DIFFERENCE BETWEEN A TALL PERSON AND A SHORT PERSON

FIG. 1.
TALL PERSON

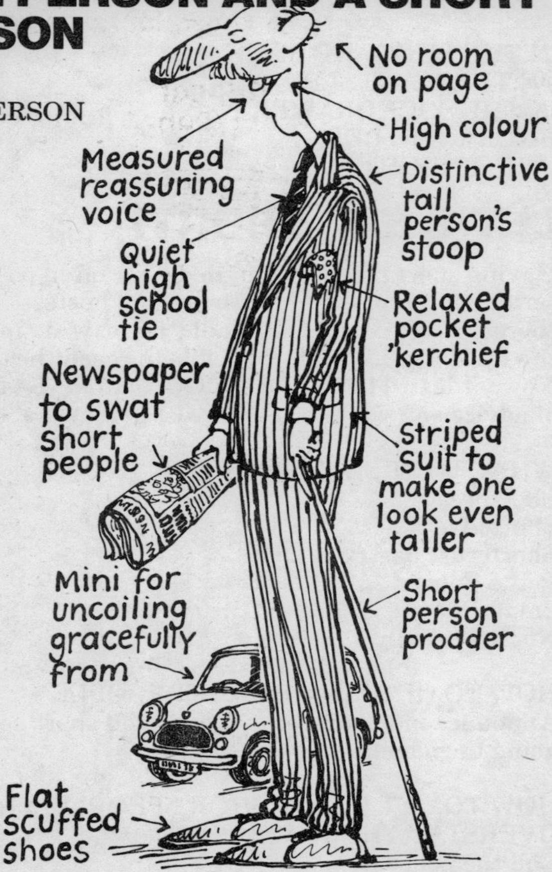

No room on page

High colour

Measured reassuring voice

Distinctive tall person's stoop

Quiet high school tie

Relaxed pocket 'kerchief

Newspaper to swat short people

Striped suit to make one look even taller

Mini for uncoiling gracefully from

Short person prodder

Flat scuffed shoes

Lots of room left on page

FIG. 2.
SHORT
PERSON

Tall car
(Range Rover)

Tall
hair
style

Low
colour

Tense

Loud
voice
to cut
through
small
talk

Angry
pocket
'kerchief

Big
black
book
to
impress

Loud
noticeable
suit

Discreetly
loud
elevated
shoes

THE PSYCHOLOGY OF THE SHORT

By our resident psychologist, Dr Fritz Anschluss

– AGGRESSION

Although nature has designed them to be less noticeable than the rest of us, short people do not like to be ignored. Their aggressive natures, though usually kept under control, can erupt without warning in the most innocuous of social situations. How often have you been peaceably discussing world affairs with a favoured short person when a chance remark, laughingly addressed to the subject of his height, has suddenly led him to lose his temper and bite you in the leg? It is no coincidence that many of the shortest people the world has ever seen have gone on to become world famous dictators and mass murderers.

– OSTENTATION

Although strictly speaking it is the social duty of the short to remain well hidden at all times, for some inexplicable reason many short people feel the need to show themselves in public. Indeed, displays of ostentation are a frequent hallmark of the squat. Loud ties, sports jackets and golfing trousers are staples of the short wardrobe, and many feel the need to compensate for their lack of size by talking loudly in restaurants, cracking bad jokes and invading Poland.

–QUERULOUSNESS

Another inexplicable personality trait of the short is a tendency to whinge. It's almost impossible to converse with a short person on any subject for long, without finding oneself on the receiving end of objections, complaints and protestations. Even the most trivial of references to the short person's risible lack of height, or a mere twenty minutes spent ridiculing his comical stature, lead invariably to completely unjustified charges of condescension, and an argument is bound to follow. The only answer is to be patient and call the police.

© Dr Fritz Anschluss

SHORT SPORTS

AN EASY-TO-FOLLOW GUIDE AS TO WHICH SPORTS ARE SUITABLE FOR THE SMALLER SPORTSMAN

UNSUITABLE:

RUNNING
JUMPING
THROWING
HURDLING
ANYTHING REALLY

SUITABLE:

SYNCHRONIZED DROWNING

TEN AMAZING SHORT FACTS

1) Attila the Hun was only 4'2" tall and yet got as far as Belgium. If he'd got any further, then we'd have seen some changes around here.

2) Over 99% of all the living organisms on this planet are under 5'2".

3) The film star Alan Ladd was so short that he had to stand on a box for most dialogue scenes.

4) Most jockeys are short.

5) Samantha Fox is even shorter.

6) Even shorter was Pauline Musters, a Dutch woman who died in New York City in 1895. She was 23 inches tall, but actually grew another inch after her death.

7) Napoleon Bonaparte had constipation.

8) Contrary to popular belief, Henri de Toulouse-Lautrec was a full five feet and one inch tall.

9) The diminutive Spanish painter Pablo Picasso had an extremely bad report card at school.

10) Dolly Parton.

THE SHORTER GUIDE TO SEX

BY A TALL SEXOLOGIST.

SEX can be a wonderful thing.

You know, there's absolutely no reason why today's short person shouldn't have as fulfilled a sex life as the next man. Just look at the Marquis de Sade.

So here now, for the uninitiated and undersized, is an easy to follow beginner's guide to staging that first vital encounter.

FINDING THE RIGHT PARTNER
1. Obtain a membership form from the dating agency.
2. When you get to the bit marked 'height', write '6 feet 3 inches'.
3. Arrange to meet your date in a dark alley.

SEDUCTION
1. Put on some soft music.
2. Slip into something comfortable.
3. Serve up a romantic dinner for two, preferably with champagne.
4. At no time switch on the light.

SEXUAL TECHNIQUE
1. Take a step ladder and position it against the bed.
2. Grasping the sides firmly with both hands, place your left foot on the bottom rung and ascend carefully.
3. At no time look down.
4. Haul yourself up and onto the bed beside your partner.
5. Fall asleep through exhaustion.

LITTLE ROCK

LACK OF SIZE IN THE MUSIC WORLD:

A searing investigation by five of the capital's most vibrant and relevant critical voices from a well known London listings magazine.

A Little In Love – Cliff Richard.
Savage and sensitively phrased piece of spry pop opportunism lamenting the doomed entanglements of the undersized in a shortist society. Richard waxes lyrical in an exhibition of almost apocalyptic bravura. The quintessential cri de coeur petit. (Andy Penge)

Little Willy – The Sweet.
Savage exposé of the short man's fundamental biological predicament. The sparse, chopping rhythmicizing of Andy Tucker's guitar justifiably sympathizes with the underendowed male. A short classic. (Dave Streatham)

Little Things Mean A Lot – Alma Cogan.
Savagely coherent manifesto for our times. Cogan's impassioned plea for a more reasoned *Kleinelebensraum* contrasts vividly with the *Weltschmerz* of bassman Lennie Dim's chugging rhythm. (Steve Camden)

Walk Tall – Val Doonican.
Savage, sneering slice of shortist innuendo making full commercial capital out of others' misfortunes. Doonican's cynical opportunism sits uneasily with his pseudo-avuncular media image, but then that's entertainment. (Anne Willesden)

Big Man In A Big House by Leroy Van Dyke.
Savage, taut, urban ballad ultimately revealed as an
ethnological forgery of elegiac proportions, as Van
Dyke is ultimately compromised by his failure to
include the diminutive minority in his domestic
arrangements. Dangerous propaganda, but then that's
life. (Pete Croydon)

SPORTSFILE
THE PORTABLE MOUNTAINEERING GUIDE

FOR THE PORTABLE MOUNTAINEER.

There are many ways in which short people can
overcome their shortness and none more so than in
the noble realm of sport. In the first of an extremely
occasional series looking at the options open to the
shorter sportsman, this week the Sportsfile
microscope focuses on mountaineering.

The compact climber is best advised to take things
easily at first. A walk to the newsagents', or a stroll
with the dog, should prepare you for your first serious
expedition. But before you set out, you must decide
which country you intend to visit. The options are
boundless. Countries such as Nepal, Switzerland or
India are perennial favourites, but for the miniature
mountaineer there can be no better starting place
than Holland. There is a very nice three foot trough to
the north west of Leidschendam, and another similar
hole near Benthuizen. When you've climbed out of
these, you should be ready to think about actually
going up.

For your next expedition we suggest an attempt on Mount Hauten, highest peak in the Utrecht basin at 9 ft. You will be able to hire guides and llamas locally, although it is easier to bring your own ropes and ice axes. Previous pygmy pioneers have recommended pitching base camp at Vreeswijk, on the banks of the Amsterdam-Rhine canal, and moving on to tackle the summit with 6 hand-picked sherpas. Allow at least a minute for the all-important final leg – but don't be complacent. On dark nights, bar gossip at the Short Mountaineers' Club bungalow turns to stories of unwary climbers caught by a gust on Houten's summit, and swept to their doom.

Now you are a seasoned climber, you can look back and smile at those early walks to the newsagents'. For now you are about to take on the sternest test of all: the mighty Dacnoje range in the Soviet Union's Ligovo Massif. Lying just to the south of Leningrad on the shores of the Baltic, the soaring ridges and craggy buttresses of these treacherous peaks ascend at one point to almost 40 ft. Here at the roof of the world, condors wheel menacingly as a breathtaking vista unfolds over Leningrad's southern suburbs. But beware; crampons, belaying pins and a 24-hour emergency back-up team are a must for the midget mountaineer who dares to do battle with Dacnoje's 12 steepling metres, for one false foothold can spell almost certain death. No elfin alpinist has ever successfully challenged Dacnoje. Maybe you will be the one to lay down this book and take on the challenge of this great peak. But learn well the lessons that spelled failure for your brave predecessors: trying to go through Leningrad airport on a half fare ticket invariably causes difficulties.

A room of my own

By a famous Northern Short Person.

A Famous Northern Short Person was born in the little Yorkshire mining town of Slaithwick in 1937.
He is still intensely proud of his northern origins, and sometimes visits there from his Hampstead flat. He is now a highly successful TV presenter.

Hullo. I'm a famous Northern Short Person. You know, I've always said that there's nobody like my old mum. Edith, or Vi as we called her for short (we were all short in our family) has always been my closet friend. When I were 18 I went down south to University and she insisted on coming with me to savour our proudest day. When t'Vice-Chancellor said, 'Who let that small boy in here?' she didn't half give him a clout round the ear 'ole. That's my Vi – or violent, as we called her for long. Or rather not for long, as she were taken away soon afterwards. I still visit her in Holloway to this day.

I vividly remember the day when I got my first pair of short trousers. They still fit. In fact I were matriculated at an early age – hence the lack of height. I wish I'd known then what I know now – which isn't a lot, but which still rings true to this very day: as my old dad used to say, 'There's nobbut grobbet when there's thribbet in the gribbet.' We still say that a lot round our way. Hardly surprising, because there's a lot of Slaithwick folk live in 'Ampstead these days – playwrights, chat show hosts, MPs and so on. Nobody really knows what it means.

Us from Slaithwick are like one big happy family. Knowing how unfriendly southern folk are, we never speak to them. But working at t'BBC, we never really meet any anyway.

Of course it's hard in t'media. TV cameras make me look short, for instance. Not as short as I look in real life, but still pretty short. Typical of t'media distortion, but it'll always be a struggle for someone with my background to fight against disadvantage. The trouble I had getting the footpedals raised on my Daimler were shockin'.

For my room I've chosen a simple, unaffected, low slung look. I don't like things too high up on the walls, as it gives the place an air of elitism: I prefer a more down to earth approach to decoration.

That's how it was back in Slaithwick, or 'Slathock' as we like to pretend it was pronounced. Even now I look out across t'Heath and my mind takes me back to my youth and t'wood-gathering in Gribblesdale (pronounced 'Grathock') and t'River Grib ('Grzb') and t'hard times we had. We may have been short, but we were happy.

(A Famous Northern Short Person was lying to Linda Scribe).

NEXT WEEK: A Sunday lunch in the room in the life of the mum in the day of Paul Daniels.

A POCKET FASHION GUIDE

For The Pocket Person

A selection of everyday fashion suggestions to enable the diminutive of stature to take their rightful place in society.

1. 'THE POUNDSTRETCHER'
    The economy sized outfit for the economy sized person, this simple but effective colour combination is easily available from most major retailers. Matching grey jacket, shorts, shirt and socks are offset by brightly striped tie and cap, enabling the wearer to be instantly recognized for what he is.

2. 'THE COUNTRYMAN'

Finding clothes can often be a problem for the shorter person, faced with the insensitivity and greed of our major department stores. But now your problems are solved, with this sturdy but stylish red and green ensemble with matching bobble hat, belt and leather boots, ideal for the outdoor life. A must for fishing expeditions, it comes complete with this modern and attractive toadstool-style seat in moulded plastic, enabling you to fit into your surroundings with ease.

Cap £599.00,
Waistcoat £499.00
Trousers £899.00,
Boots £1039.00 from
Ricardo Nain of Bond Street.
Toadstool direct from
Nabot of Milano
price £2379.99.

3. 'HOMME DE NUIT'

Evening wear need no longer present obstacles to
a successful social life with this elegantly cut slim
navy coat, matching crescent headwear and knee-
length PVC boots. Gold buttons and epaulettes
complete this sophisticated collection, and there is
a special recessed pocket to keep your right hand
warm on those long winter retreats.

Coat £5199.00, Hat £1379.00 Boots £2049.00 from
Mioches of South Molton Street. One way ticket to
Moscow from Intourist of Regent Street.

HOLIDAYS FOR SHORT PEOPLE

Taking your short person on holiday can prove a major headache: it's never easy to find the right resort, with shorter beaches, shallower swimming pools and lower restaurant tables. The half-pint holiday maker is constantly at risk from passing tall people, whether they be kicking sand in his face, stealing his ice-lolly or simply puncturing his inflatable duck-shaped rubber ring. In response to the increased demand for reduced holiday opportunities, we have compiled a list of suitable short breaks with facilities for the elfin excursionist.

PIGMY PARADISE

An exciting African jaunt to the land where everyone's a short person. Your little companion will be able to gambol and romp through the jungle with his new found flesh-eating pals. Meals provided (subject to size of tour party).

HAMELIN HIKE

Sample the medieval atmosphere of this charming German village on a guided musical mystery tour. Devised mainly for children, but with special facilities for short people and rats.

HAMPTON COURT HOLIDAY

Your short person will be a-mazed as he is airlifted into the middle of the famous Hampton Court Maze. High hedges ensure he will not be able to find his way out easily. Days of fun!

ABRIDGED CLASSICS

For the abridged reader.

The home of every short person is never without a well-stocked library of mind-improving weighty tomes: literature pervades every aspect of the short person's life. Whether painting the ceiling, looking over the garden gate or reaching up to the dinner table, what could be more solid than a good thick pile of books to stand on?.

This convenient practice can lead to social embarrassment, however. What to do if your friends actually canvas your opinion on these great works? Or, for that matter, ask you to lift them up? But fear not – THE SHORT BOOK has the answer to all your problems, with these specially abridged versions of famous classics from literature. Drawn up by a celebrated short Professor of English, each of these versions fully captures the essence of the famous original – so YOU don't have to read it.

1. **1984** By George Orwell
   'It was a bright cold day in April, and the clocks were striking thirteen. Winston Short, his chin nuzzled into his knees in an effort to escape the vile wind, slipped quickly through the glass doors. On each landing, opposite the lift shaft, the poster with the squat face gazed from the wall: "LITTLE BROTHER IS WATCHING YOU" the caption beneath it ran.'

2. **Treasure Island** By Robert Louis Stevenson
   'Ay, ay, mateys' said Short John Silver, who was standing by, with his crutch under his arm, and at

once broke out in the air and words I knew so well
– 'Fifteen men on the short man's chest – yo ho ho
and a bottle of tizer!'

3. **Small Expectations** By Charles Dickens
'Joe and I gasped, and looked at one another. "I am
instructed to communicate to him," said Mr
Jaggers, throwing his fingers at me sideways, "that
he will come into a modest property. Further, that
it is the desire of the present possessor of that
property, that he be immediately removed from his
present sphere of life and from this place, and be
brought up as a short person – in a word, as a
young fellow of small expectations." '

4. **The Pocket Gatsby** By F. Scott Fitzgerald
'In my shorter and more vulnerable years my
father gave me some advice that I've been turning
over in my mind ever since. "Whenever you feel
like criticizing anyone", he told me, "just
remember that they're bigger than you!" '

Simply memorize these easy-to-remember passages,
and you too will be able to hold your own at dinner
parties, bar mitzvahs, boy's brigade meetings and
social occasions. Before long you will be a regular in
London Literary Society, asked to contribute to *Books
and Bookmen* and invited to lunch with A.N. Wilson.
And all thanks to THE SHORT BOOK.

Next week: The Bronté's WUTHERING DEPTHS plus
John Osborne's LOOK UP IN ANGER.

SELF-PROTECTION FOR THE SHORT

These are dangerous times in which to be short. The nation's average height is rising rapidly, while the height of short people remains at a standstill. Everywhere, tall people roam the streets unchecked.

In these perilous climes, it is increasingly vital for the short person to adopt a wide range of defensive techniques against potential predators. Kendo, Kung Fu, Jujitsu and Char Siu Bun* are all becoming popular with the tiny. Here is a selection of basic defensive methods for you to practise in the privacy of your own home.

A. KARATE
1. Raise your right arm over your head.
2. Grasp your left foot with right wrist.
3. Cry: 'Eeeeeeaaaiioouuaarggh!'
   (Not difficult in the light of 1. & 2. above)
4. While your tall assailant is distracted, bite him on the ankle and run away.

B. KENDO
1. Grasp the kendo stick firmly with both hands.
2. Ask, 'Would you mind holding this please?'
3. While your tall assailant is distracted, bite him on the ankle and run away.

C. CHINESE FOOD
1. Take your tall assailant to a Chinese restaurant.
2. Ask to see the menu.
3. While your tall assailant is making up his mind, nip under the table, bite him on the ankle and run away.

   * A form of roast pork pastry available in Chinese restaurants.

SELF-PROTECTION AGAINST THE SHORT

1. Buy some metal socks.

FAIRY TALES FOR SHORT CHILDREN*

By Margery Squit.

It is a sad fact that few traditional fairy tales were written with the short in mind. All too often, tall handsome princes rescued tall slim princesses from tall towers and lived happily ever after, leaving those such as goblins, elves, dwarves etc. to return to their holes in the ground. THE SHORT BOOK has now endeavoured to remedy this deficiency with a series of specially commissioned fairy tales, aimed specifically at the reduced reader.

DWARF AND THE SEVEN SNOW WHITES
'Mirror, mirror on the wall, who is the shortest of them all?' asked the Dwarf Queen. 'Not you for a start, shorthouse,' laughed the Mirror condescendingly, 'the seven snow whites are much more dinky.' The queen snarled and went out to the Whites' cottage in the woods dressed as a humble washerwoman, armed with a basket of poison apples; but unfortunately the snow whites easily saw through

*Most children are short.

her disguise. So the disgruntled queen had their cottage bombed out of existence.

THE FROG PRINCE

There once was a prince so short and ugly that he was indistinguishable from a frog. Down at the pond one day, one of his froggy pals revealed to him that only a kiss from the beautiful Princess Anorexa would break the spell and banish his warts, bulging eyes, green skin and croaking voice forever. Being gullible, he lay in wait for her in the forest of grass that was his home, and one day was rewarded when he espied the fair princess skipping through the trees. He hopped out of the undergrowth and was just about to present himself to her when she inadvertently trod on him and he bled to death.

THE UGLY DUCKLING

There once was an ugly duckling, in stature all stubby and brown. How the other ducks laughed at his lack of size! Then one day he woke to find that he had become a beautiful swan. He leapt up and flew for all the world to see and admire, but unfortunately got sucked into the jet intake of a passing Boeing 747.

SLEEPING BEAUTY

And so the short prince came to the final bush. Beyond the last thicket stood the enchanted castle, that had lain dormant for a thousand years, the castle in which slept the beautiful Princess Pelva. Summoning up his last ounce of strength, he raised his penknife and swept the bush away forever.

'Oi, wot are you doing here, shorthouse?' spake a large bearded labourer. 'Bog off, squitty, this is private property.'

'But prithee sire, surely this is the site of the castle of wise King Eggwulf, home of the beauteous sleeping Princess Pelva?' asked the Prince, almost in tears. The Irishman's tone mellowed.
'No mate. The M25's going through here.'
The Prince wept and threw himself into a cement mixer.

THE THREE LITTLE PIGS

There once were three little pigs. One little piggy built a house of straw, but a tall wolf came along and blew it down in the night. The second little piggy built a home of sticks, but the same tall wolf set fire to it. The third house, however, was built of stone. Immediately all the pigs claimed on their insurance, wrote letters to the papers, applied for rebuilding grants and generally behaved in a short fashion. The poor public-spirited wolf was hounded by the press and forced to flee the country, while the pigs went on to become Mayor and successfully carried out a series of major local government frauds.

LITTLE RED RIDING HOOD AND THE BIG BAD WOLF

An enjoyable snack for the wolf, which partly compensated for his ordeal at the hands of the pigs. The CID never found the bones, but they did arrest the pigs on a tip-off from the wolf, who lived happily ever after.

AM I SHORT?

That's the question short people everywhere are
asking themselves. And the answer comes back with a
resounding 'YES'. But never mind them, what about
you? Are *you* short? Teams of hack journalists
working through their lunch breaks have devised the
following comprehensive test of ideals, attitudes and
lifestyles.

1. Your favourite film star is
    (a) Clint Eastwood
    (b) Meryl Streep
    (c) Robert Redford
    (d) R2D2

2. When you grow up, you want to be
    (a) A fireman
    (b) An engine driver
    (c) An astronaut
    (d) Emperor of France

3. Your favourite dance is
    (a) The waltz
    (b) The foxtrot
    (c) The funky chicken
    (d) The limbo

4. In the pub, you catch the barman's eye, and he
    greets you with a cheery
    (a) 'Yes sir, what can I get you?'
    (b) 'Hullo Reg, pint of the usual?'
    (c) 'It's what your right arm's for.'
    (d) 'I'm sorry sonny. I can't serve you with a glass

of lemonade until I've seen your birth
certificate.'

5. What is your attitude to Adolf Hitler:
   (a) A monstrous blot on the past
   (b) Best forgotten
   (c) Made the trains run on time
   (d) May not have been very nice, but at least he
   was short.

6. Your favourite 'Page 3 Girl' is
   (a) Samantha Fox
   (b) Debbee Ashby
   (c) Gillian de Terville
   (d) Lester Piggott

7. Your favourite fifth century mass-murderer was:
   (a) Odoacer
   (b) Theodoric
   (c) Attila
   (d) Lester the Hun

Well, are you short?
Mostly a's, b's, and c's: No.
Mostly d's: Well, what do you think?

WAYS TO GET TALLER

A GUIDE FOR THE COMPRESSED

Stand in the rain.

Tell Irish jokes in an
Irish pub.

LET'S PARLER SHORT!

Short people have a confusing battery of private words and phrases, each with their own special meaning. Now THE SHORT BOOK lifts the lid on this secretive language to enable you to slip inconspicuously into short society.

SHORT CIRCUIT	A race meeting for the smaller of stature.
SHORTHOUSE	Kennel.
SHORT ODDS	Paul Daniels and Ronnie Corbett.
SMALL TALK	The David Hamilton Show.
SHORTCOMINGS	The sex life of the undersized.
SHORTCHANGED	Diminutive transsexual.
SHORTHAND	Midget farm labourer.
SHORTFALL	A tiddler falling off a pavement.
LYING LOW	Mendacious dwarf.
IT'S A SMALL WORLD	No it isn't.

YES! IT'S THE
GLORIOUS TWELFTH

By 'Gamekeeper'

'Yes! It's the glorious twelfth' – magic words which bring a flush of excitement to the faces of sportsmen and women the length and breadth of Britain. It's a time for unpacking the trusty spring-loader, a time for dusting down the beloved deerstalker and shooting tweeds, a time for settling old scores. The scent of the heather, the whip of the fresh highland breeze, the ruddy glow of the crackling embers in the grate at the end of a hard day's bloodletting: all these will be familiar images to the doughty countryman, as he crank starts the trusty old two-seater Austin Maestro for the trip north to the braes and banks he knows so well. Will fortune smile this year, or will the will o' the wisp deal the wrong hand of the dice, as the stout-booted backwoodsman traipses home down the craggy glen past the salmon leap where the sparkling waters play? 'Yes, it's the glorious twelfth' – magic words which mean only one thing. It's the start of the short person season!

1. Trapping
Flushing a fugitive short person out of the heather can be a difficult task. A variety of specialist traps are available, from the simplest snare to a more satisfying cast-iron trap with powerful steel-sprung jaws. The master huntsman, however, prefers to pit his wits against his diminutive prey in a psychological battle of move and counter-move: he will aim to lure the short person towards a spot where

44

he has already dug a concealed hole, some two feet in depth.

2. Shooting
Have your gillies prepare a short person for the day's sport by affixing cardboard wings to him, liberally coated with glue and feathers. As the beaters prod him out of the undergrowth with their sticks, you and your friends will be lying in wait with your trusty sawn-off shotguns.

3. Hunting
The oldest sport of all. Have your short person immersed in chicken stock prior to the day's entertainment, then release him. Thirty seconds later, release the pack of gigantic half-starved crazed mastiffs. It is unlikely that you will see him again.

'Gamekeeper' says: 'There's nae whinnie when there's grinnie in the binnie.'

FIVE SHORT PEOPLE THAT SHOOK THE WORLD!

By Lynda Lee-Leslie.

The pages of history are crammed with short people, mainly because they don't take up much room!! Let's raise a cheer for five of the guys and gals that galvanized the globe with their glorious goings-on.

ALEXANDER POPE
At 4'6", portable Al Pope was the pigmy poet who really packed a punch. 'A little learning is a dangerous thing' quipped Al. Well, we're certainly learning from you, little 'un!

FRANCIS OF ASSISSI
At 5'1", Fabulous Frankie was the stunted saint that saved the flora and fauna from the flood – The birds and the bees were a-buzzin' when Fantastic Fran and his ark were in town. I'll go on board two by two anytime, Franny-baby!!

NIKITA KRUSCHEV
At 5'3", Nicky was the Dinky Dictator who nearly dropped us in it! The miniaturized maniac and his midget missile crisis sure had us shakin' in our snow shoes for a while back there!

THE MARQUIS de SADE
At 5'3", the minimal Marquis with his saucy sadism had the world a-whippin' and a whackin' until the tall people came and took him away – Now he's all tied up!!

HARRY PILLING

Little Harry Pilling was the shortest player in the County Championship. But pint-sized Pilling really piled on the runs despite the Lancashire rain. At 5'1", he must have shrunk.

YOU TOO CAN BE SHORT!

EXCLUSIVE – ONLY IN THE SHORT BOOK

Yes, the exciting world of the short can also be yours. No more bumping your head in doorways, or people mistaking you for John Cleese. Now you too can lose those vital inches and experience the unique lifestyle that is short.

The most common cause of restricted growth amongst the otherwise normal, healthy and socially acceptable is *heredity*, and so a useful short cut to life at knee height is to ensure that your parents are themselves fairly miniscule. This could be quite tricky to arrange, but the following guide will assist you in your choice:

UNSUITABLE PARENTS
Basketball Players
West Indian Fast Bowlers
Policemen
Darth Vader

SUITABLE PARENTS
Jockeys
Japanese Businessmen
Sylvester Stallone
Short People Generally

If heredity is a problem – and it could be if you are already born – why not try *world leadership*, another popular shortener? There are snags involved – inevitable defeat for example.

But did Napoleon complain, as he fought his way down to become the most powerful dictator Europe has ever known? Of course he did, but then he was short.

There are easier ways, though. All sorts of modern habits have a suppressant effect on the growth hormones, most famously *smoking*. But other less well known stunters can be just as effective as tobacco, such as drug abuse, self-abuse, alcoholism and the shameless performance of magic tricks on television. Some of these will render you not only short, but probably bald, squeaky and extremely rich as well.

© Rick T. Sportswear.

SHORT PEOPLE IN LITERATURE

TOM THUMB
GULLIVER
NODDY
MRS PEPPERPOT
RAGGLE TAGGLE THE MAGIC PIXIE
PAUL DANIELS

ORGANIZATIONS FOR SHORT PEOPLE

A brief rundown of organizations where the short person can meet like-minded and like-heighted people in a convivial context.

The Boy Scout movement.

The Ray Moore appreciation society.

The Jockey Club.

The Magic Circle.

The Munchkins.

The Third Reich.

THE SMALL SCREEN

By Pearl N. Dean.

It is a sad reflection on the overcautious nature of the Hollywood dream factory that cinema moguls and directors have all too often played down the importance of the short person in the movies. Short screen stars such as Alan Ladd and Audie Murphy had to suffer the indignity of perching on an orange box, Prince-Charles-style, while their co-stars were frequently reduced to standing in a trench. Even now, fine actors such as Sylvester Stallone are only allowed on screen to get punched repeatedly. Stars of international calibre such as Mickey Rooney were kept away from romantic leading parts by sheer prejudice and a sordid desire to maximize profits. But the celluloid picture has not always been such a bleak one. A number of pioneering stars, producers and directors have been beavering away down the years to create a distinct genre – the small screen epic. Here, then, are some of the significant stunted landmarks in the history of the cinema.

MIDGE ON THE RIVER KWAI
Postwar David Lean tragedy centered around a group of brave and ingenious Japanese short people who fool British soldiers into building a bridge for them. Unfortunately a lot of tall people come along at the end and blow it up.

SOME LIKE IT SQUAT
Heartwarming comedy by Billy Wilder (Director of the SEVEN YEAR TITCH) showing that even

someone as short as Tony Curtis can get Marilyn Monroe.

CHARGE OF THE SLIGHT BRIGADE
Fine piece of social realism by Tony Richardson thinly disguised as a move towards the epic. The callous destruction of the glittering Slight Brigade is in fact an allegory for the wholesale massacre of short people in society at large.

TIDDLER ON THE ROOF
Another manifesto for the short condition, this time a musical investigation by Norman Jewison into restricted housing availability.

WHINGEING IN THE RAIN
Seminal short complaint about how much more dangerous a puddle can be to the smaller of stature.

LOGAN'S RUNT
Definitive 1976 sci-fi thriller concerning an idealized future society where anyone who passes 5'6" is automatically killed off. The diminutive Michael York plays a misguided assassin who destroys his own utopia for the love of a tall person (Jenny Agutter).

SHORT PEOPLE AROUND BRITAIN

Issued by the

English Shortist Board

As the legend of the leprechaun shows, there is a long tradition of midgets and dwarves in the Emerald Isle. Petulant, peevish, and generally up to their knees in mud, few people could be so squat and crotchety as the Irish.

In few places are short people so short as those in Scotland. Years of peat cutting and cold winds blowing around the exposed knees have taken their toll on the downwardly mobile Scots. Hence their drunken irascibility.

Slim and elegant, tall and sophisticated, immeasurably superior in every respect, the Englishman is driven to his club in a pre-war Bentley, to be met by a team of liveried retainers. On the way, if he is feeling magnanimous, he will toss pie crusts and other titbits to grateful short people from other countries who line the gutters of his fair city. Such short people as there are in England may be dismissed out of hand.

Few short people are more argumentative and objectionable than those in Wales. Long days in low mine tunnels and subsequent lack of exposure to sunlight have led to a general shortening of temper as well as height.

PYGMY PUZZLE PAGE

A selection of posers and brain-teasers for the portable puzzler.

SPOT THE SHORT PERSON.
Hidden somewhere in this picture is a short person.
Can you spot where he is, chums?

```
Y Q S Q U A T
L I L O W E E
D S M A L L G
D H C T I T D
I O P Y S T I
F R A W D I M
Z T I N Y L X
D A N I E L S
```

SHORTWORD

How many words can you spot with short connotations in the 'shortword'? Going up, down, across, backwards or diagonally.

Answers below.

CELEBRITY ANAGRAMS

Yes, pals, here are some of your favourite short people from film, television and 19th century history – but they're all mixed up.

Can you unravel them?

1. 2RD2
2. ALPU NADIELS
3. SAMATHNA XOF
4. PANONEOL
5. ROVILLE THE DUKC
6. LEON DEMONDS

SHORTWORD ANSWERS: 16
Dwarf. Tiny. Short. Small. Titch. Squat. Little. Lil'.
Midget. Itsy. Wee. Fiddly. Low. Pain. Daniels. AWAC
(Advanced Missile Early Warning System sometimes
piloted by short people).

55

SHORT MART

A SELECTION OF PRODUCTS FOR THE DISCERNING SHORTIE

Spare those bathtime blushes with this easy-to-fit

Sink Diving Board

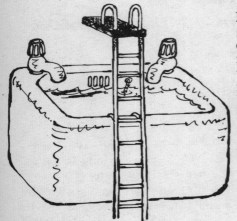

Never again the embarrassment of not being able to reach the sink on wash days. This miniaturized springboard in finest Swedish pine fits any sink, enabling you to leap easily to bathtime doom. Sorry, fun.

ONLY £49.99

56

Avoid mealtime embarrassment with this new design in posture planning. No longer will you suffer the shame of not being able to reach dinner with this unique

RAISED SEATING ENVIRONMENT

Specially designed for the smaller stature, this amazing scientific breakthrough has been specially constructed with a pigmy posture in mind.

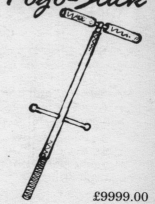

controls

(Kindergarten Surplus £99.99)

Yes! It's the new

Public House Pogo-Stick

Say goodbye to saloon bar humiliation with this revolutionary breakthrough by Norwegian scientists. No longer will your lack of height prevent you seeing over the bar to catch the barman's eye – this Pogo stick enables you to bound vertically into a conspicuous purchasing position.

£9999.00

Get that winter tan with the

SAUNA-MICROWAVE

all in one tanner and roaster!

Toast your toes and bronze your body with this new
sixty-second sauna sensation!! Also heats up pies,
cornish pasties, pot noodles, 'Frankies' individual
hot-dogs, sausages etc.
Designed exclusively for the short.
As recommended by Jimmy Tarbuck
(Pub surplus).

Walk tall with the new

"PORTABLE PROMENADER"

Fashion walking accessory. Our easy-to-assemble two part kit clips together to become a completely unnoticeable height extension unit in flexible Filipino beechwood. Fool your friends!

ONLY £399.99 + balancing pole.

End shopping misery! Carrier bags will become a thing of the past with the new

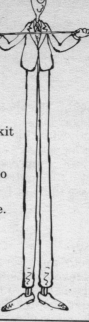

"SHOPSHORT"

grocery transporter.

Fashioned in elegant stainless steel with hand-tooled plastic handles, this hard wearing trolley-style conveyance will revolutionize your shopping habits!

Every 'Shopshort' comes complete with a special travelling compartment for the dinky purchaser. Simply give the nearest assistant an enormous tip – he will do your shopping for you and then propel you out to the car park where your Reliant Robin is parked.

EXERCISING THE SHORT

A series of exercises to keep your short person
fighting fit and glowing with health, as especially
devised by Dr. Karl Plinth of Stockholm's famous
Shrimphuset.

1. Ripping up Telephone Directories
   Your short person will be able to build up his
   strength with this simple tearing exercise. Start
   him at a page a day – it's unlikely he'll be able to
   manage any more – and carry on until every page
   has been torn out: then buy him another one. This
   will keep him out from under your feet for a few
   years.

2. Arm Wrestling
   Buy your short person an old record player, and put
   on his favourite Nik Kershaw disc. The aim of the
   exercise is to see if he can prevent the record arm
   reaching the middle. Hopefully this will also make
   the record unplayable.

3. Weight Training
   The short person runs round the room while you
   drop weights on his head. The exercise value is
   minimal, but it's jolly good fun.

4. Going Down To The Shops.
   When in need of extra groceries or household
   goods, what better exercise for your short person

than to dispatch him to the shops? Untie him, give him a shopping list and not quite enough money, and remember to ask for your change when he returns.

(Dr. Karl Plinth is now appearing in 'Snow White and the Seven Dwarves' at the Fjord Theatre, Tromso.)

MICROGRAPHY

A selection of further reading for Pigmophiles and anyone who wishes to investigate the short ethic in greater detail. Most of these works will be found on the lower shelves of your local library.

LITTLE WOMEN By Louisa M. Alcott
(Searing, realistic work on the lives of four sisters who lose their innocence along with their height.).

BRIEF LIVES By John Aubrey
(The best type).

GULLIVER'S TRAVELS By Jonathan Swift
(Ostensibly a children's book; in fact, a gruelling allegory on the short condition, where a tall person learns just what it's like to be pint-sized).

MEIN KAMPF by Adolf Hitler (Well he *was* short).

THE NOEL EDMUNDS LATE LATE BREAKFAST SHOW GOLDEN BOOK OF RUBBISH
By 117 uncredited researchers.
(Zappy, snappy, pappy, fun book. Ignore the camera tricks – in real life, they don't come much shorter than Noel!!!).

THE SHORTER ENGLISH DICTIONARY
(Gripping unputdownable stuff. Much better than the longer one).

SMALL IS BEAUTIFUL By E.F. Schumacher
(A study of economics as if short people mattered).

LITTLE DORRIT By Charles Dickens
(Rather long and heavy, this. Get the Reader's Digest
shortened version).

IT'S A FUNNY GAME By Little Harry Pilling
(Nuff said).

These books are also available by mail order in
specialist lightweight paper editions. Send your
cheques to:

La Banque Internationale des Hommes Petits
Humeureux,
Zurich, Switzerland.

Don't worry, we'll fill in the amount.

AFTERWORD

BY AN EVEN SHORTER FAMOUS PERSON THAN
LAST TIME.

Hullo. I'm an even shorter person than last time. I'd
just like to express the wish that you've enjoyed this
brief foray into the short idiom, and that you will be